Assisted Human Reproduction
Facts and Ethical Issues

Bishops' Committee on Bioethics

VERITAS

...ications

...et

Veritas Publications
7/8 Lower Abbey St,
Dublin 1

...yright © 2000, Bishops' Committee on Bioethics

ISBN 1 85390 596 8

Design by Colette Dower
Photography by Valerie O'Sullivan
Printed in the Republic of Ireland by Betaprint Ltd, Dublin

Table of Contents

Chapter 1
Assisted Human Reproduction: Establishing Principles
Scientific Research Involving Human Embryos   7
The Nature and Scope of this Document   7
The Right to Life and Bodily Integrity   8
The Right to an Identity of Origin   10
The Essential Meaning of Human Sexuality   12
Conscience   13

Chapter 2
Assisted Human Reproduction: Current Practice
A. Investigation for and Diagnosis of Infertility   17
B. Responding to Infertility   17
C. Curative Therapy   18
    1. NaProTechnology   18
    2. Surgery   18
    3. Drug Treatment   18
D. Circumventive Therapy   19
    1. *In Vitro* Fertilisation   19
    2. Intra-Cytoplasmic Sperm Injection (ICSI)   21
    3. Embryo Donation   21
    4. Gamete Intra-Fallopian Tube Transfer (GIFT)   21
    5. Egg Donation   22
    6. Surrogacy   22
    7. Assisted Insemination by Husband (AIH) and Intra-Uterine Insemination (IUI)   22
    8. Artificial Insemination by Donor (AID)   23
    9. Testicular Biopsy   23

Chapter 3
Assisted Human Reproduction: Ethical Evaluation of Current Practice
A. Curative Therapy   27
    1. NaProTechnology   27
    2. Surgery   27
    3. Drug Treatment   27

	B.	Circumventive Therapy	28
		1. *In Vitro* Fertilisation and Embryo Transfer	28
		2. Intra-Cytoplasmic Sperm Injection (ICSI)	31
		3. Embryo Donation	31
		4. Gamete Intra-Fallopian Tube Transfer (GIFT)	32
		5. Assisted Insemination by Husband (AIH) and Intra-Uterine Insemination (IUI)	32
		6. Artificial Insemination by Donor (AID)	33
		7. Ovum Donation	33
		8. Surrogacy	34
		9. Assisted Reproductive Therapy and Marriage	34

Chapter 4
Healthcare Policy and Assisted Human Reproduction

1.	Legislating for AHR	37
2.	Funding	37
3.	The Priority of Prevention and Cure	39

Appendix

Notes	43
Select Bibliography	45

Chapter 1

Assisted Human Reproduction

Establishing Principles

Scientific Research Involving Human Embryos

Research into human embryos began in Britain in the 1950s. It was hoped that the research would help doctors

- to understand and prevent genetic disorders, such as Spina Bifida and Down's Syndrome, and
- to develop ways of helping infertile couples to have a child.

It was 1978 before the first child was born by the process of *In vitro* fertilisation. In the twenty years since then, the research has continued, and assisted human reproduction services, offering IVF and other procedures, have been set up all over the world.

Like many other branches of modern medicine, assisted human reproduction depends on the close collaboration of scientists and healthcare professionals. While these share a common goal, they approach this goal from different directions. The primary concern of the healthcare professional must always be the well-being of the patient as a person. By contrast, scientific research is primarily concerned with gaining information and delivering results. The scientist wants to know what is possible, and how it can be achieved. What is possible may also be morally good, but not always.

As in other areas of research, so in the case of biomedical research, scientific developments have enormous implications for people, and for society. Often it is only when research is well under way, or even completed, and we have discovered what is possible, that we begin to ask ourselves whether this is good or appropriate, and how its use should be regulated. If the well-being and dignity of the patient as a person is to remain central, it is essential that questions about the meaning, or the human implications of certain research or treatment should not be put to one side, while all the focus is on the asking of scientific questions. In the case of assisted human reproduction, as well as the couple being treated, every embryo must be regarded as a new human life, and respected as such.

The Nature and Scope of this Document

No reasonable person would question the very natural desire of a couple to have a child who flows, as it were, from their own love. One can only imagine the

Assisted Human Reproduction: Facts and Ethical Issues

disappointment, and even perhaps the sense of failure, that many couples experience when it is not possible for them to have a child. Against that background, assisted human reproduction therapy, in its various forms, must seem like a god-send.

This document, without wishing to minimise the importance of the many complex emotions involved, sets out to propose some fundamental principles that must be taken into account, by all those concerned, when making decisions about the treatment of infertility.

The Catholic Church has a particular vision of human sexuality, which is rooted in the understanding of the human person found in the Scriptures, as well as in the natural law. This document is addressed primarily to those who consider themselves members of the Catholic Church. We are confident that it will also be welcomed by many others who share our faith in the God of Creation. Similarly, there will be many who, although they may not be religious, will share the belief (which traces its roots to the philosophy of ancient Greece), that our human reason enables us to discern a law written in nature itself, which leads us to recognise what is good.

Assisted human reproduction gives rise to a number of issues that have to do with fundamental human rights, issues such as respect for human life, and respect for the family. In exploring questions such as these, the bishops intend to engage in dialogue, not just with members of the Catholic Church, but with Irish society as a whole.

The Right to Life and Bodily Integrity
One of the fundamental rights promulgated in the Universal Declaration of Human Rights[1] is the right of every human being to life and bodily integrity. Although the right to life finds a particularly strong foundation in Christian faith, it is a right that is acknowledged by people of all faiths and none. In the final analysis, respect for the right to life is reciprocal in nature. My requirement that my right to life should be respected by others, logically implies that I should afford a similar respect to their right to life.

At what point should this respect begin? Biologically speaking, life is a continuum. Genetically speaking, however, and in terms of philosophy, each human life has a beginning, a point at which this distinct individual comes into being. Genetic science has contributed to our awareness that each human being has a unique identity, related to but distinct from either of his/her parents. The obligation to respect life begins at the point when individual human life begins, or even when there is a reasonable possibility that it may have begun.

It is clear that, once fertilisation has been completed, there is – at the very least – a reasonable possibility that a new human being exists, and this brings with it an obligation of respect. It is clearly in the interests of justice and the common good that this obligation should be reflected in civil law. Recent embryological studies indicate that fertilisation is a process rather than an instantaneous event. The beginning of cell division marks the end of this process. The stage prior to cell division is described as the pronuclear stage. The question has been raised in recent discussions as to whether the same respect should be afforded to the human pro-nucleus, as is afforded to the embryo at the two-cell stage and later.[2]

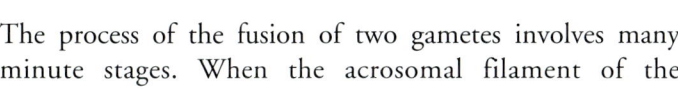

The process of the fusion of two gametes involves many minute stages. When the acrosomal filament of the spermatozoon touches the surface of the ovum, and the protective membranes are penetrated,

> the parts of the plasmalemma of the spermatozoon and the egg, outside the zone of contact, fuse together in a continuous sheet. The cytoplasmic contents of the two gametes are now in direct continuity. Although the shape of the spermatozoon may yet be distinguishable, the two gametes have at this stage become one single cell.[3]

The pronucleus is clearly far more than a sperm cell and an ovum. It has an organic unity and is, as one unit, oriented towards on-going development. It is also, of course, biologically human. It has been possible for some years to successfully freeze the human pro-nucleus. It is worth noting, however, that it has proved significantly more difficult to freeze the ovum without destroying it.[4] This simple fact serves to demonstrate that, by the pro-nuclear stage, very significant development has already taken place, as a result of the fusion of the sperm and the ovum. It has become a single organism, and has already begun to develop.

Once fertilisation is complete, the organism has become a human being. There is

Assisted Human Reproduction: Facts and Ethical Issues

nothing else it can be. It continues to develop and grow, of course. But all development or change necessarily involves some continuity – something in which the change takes place. This 'something' is the human individual. It has its own genetically unique body. It has its own substantial form, the human soul, which is its first principle of life. It is this principle of life that facilitates and directs the development of the person throughout the lifetime of the organism.[5]

In the final analysis, where doubt exists on the level of fact, the integrity of conscience requires that the presumption be in favour of life. The classical example often cited is as follows: if a hunter hears a rustling noise in the bushes, and is unsure whether it is a deer or another human being, he must assume it is a human being, until such time as he can establish that it is not. Similarly, we may accept the argument that there is scientific uncertainty as to the precise moment when an individual human life begins. That uncertainty, however, does not remove the obligation of care and respect for what certainly has the potential to become, *and may already be*, a distinct human individual.

The Right to an Identity of Origin

The Universal Declaration of Human Rights acknowledges the right of men and women 'to marry and to found a family'.[6] This is best understood as a right *not to be prevented* from founding a family. It is not an absolute right to have children. As is clear from the same article of the Declaration, the family as 'the fundamental group unit of society' is entitled to protection. This would include protection from any form of reproductive therapy which, however well-intentioned, would have the effect of weakening the bonds of family.

Parenthood is not simply a matter of life-giving. There is an essential natural link between the life-giving role of parents, and their responsibility to care for and educate their young. This on-going responsibility of parents is not exclusive to the human species, but is found to a greater or lesser degree in very many species of birds and animals. In human nature, however, the period of time between birth and maturity is relatively longer than in any other species. The process of growth to maturity involves far more than mere survival. The human child is dependent on his/her parents for emotional, spiritual, social, and moral formation. Inevitably some elements of the parental role will be delegated to others (e.g., teachers), but the primary responsibility rests with the parents. The only justification for permanently handing this responsibility over to others would be the incapacity of a parent to respond adequately to the needs of the child.

In recent years we have witnessed the phenomenon of a great many adopted people who have wanted to discover who their genetic parents are, and even to establish a relationship of some kind with these parents. This phenomenon should not be seen in any sense as a denial of the goodness and generosity of adoptive parents. It is simply an affirmation of the fact that, as autonomous human individuals, our identity and our self-understanding is, to a significant extent, dependent on our genetic origins.

Why should we assume that this desire to know who one's natural parents are, is any less likely to surface in people who are born following the donation of sperm, or ovum, or both. The right to this information, later in life, might well be found to conflict with the practice of guaranteeing anonymity to donors.

Like all fundamental human needs, the need for on-going parenting, and for a recognisable identity of origin, gives rise to a corresponding right. This right has always been acknowledged by the Church, and is expressed in the document *Donum vitae:*

> The child has the right to be conceived, carried in the womb, brought into the world and brought up within marriage: it is through the secure and recognised relationship to his own parents that the child can discover his own identity and achieve his own proper human development.[7]

While the primary consideration must be the good of the individual child, the close connection between genetic parenthood and the responsibility of care is also in the interests of society, and this has long been recognised in our social legislation. A stable family unit, founded on a commited relationship, plays a role of fundamental importance to society. It is in the family first and foremost that children discover their identity and their individuality, that they learn respect for themselves and for others. It is in the family that cultural and moral values are learnt. Any procedure that undermines the unity and integrity of the family also damages the fabric of society, because the institution of the family is the foundation on which society is built.

Assisted Human Reproduction: Facts and Ethical Issues

The Essential Meaning of Human Sexuality

Human sexuality is designed in such a way that the coming together of man and woman *as one flesh* is both an expression of intimacy and self-giving *and* the privileged context in which new life begins. This is not simply a statement of religious belief. It is evident from any realistic reflection on the facts of biology, physiology, and human psychology.

It is arguable that the term *reproduction* is not the most appropriate term to describe what happens when a new human being comes into existence. The concept of *reproduction* captures well enough the biological dimension of human generation, but it is not really capable of expressing the mystery of how man and woman, through their own human loving, co-operate with the creative action of God. An alternative term, which may better express this personalistic dimension of human life-giving, is *pro-creation*.

Technology has an important contribution to make to almost every area of modern medicine, including the treatment of infertility. There is a valid distinction to be made, however, between situations in which technology plays a supporting role, and situations in which technology becomes dominant. In every area of healthcare, people express their frustration and discomfort when they experience the intrusiveness of technology.

This is no less the case where the treatment of infertility is concerned. The more dominant technology becomes, the more the personalistic dimension of human sexuality tends to be separated from the act of life-giving, and the more easily the creative act of God is obscured. We have to ask ourselves whether a procedure that is completely controlled, that tends towards predictability, and that may also be highly selective, is a true expression of what human life-giving is about. Is the intrusiveness of technology too high a price to pay?

Parents are naturally proud of their children, anxious about their children, and sometimes disappointed in their children. In the final analysis, however, children are not for their parents. Their value is in themselves, and in their vocation as the sons and daughters of God who created them. There is a risk, in all our relationships, that we seek to possess the ones we love. It is arguable that this risk is increased when technology becomes dominant, because the child who is born has been carefully planned, with the outlay of considerable emotional energy and economic resources. What if the end result doesn't measure up to our hopes and expectations?

The desire for success, both professionally and on a human level, means that doctors and scientists are also liable to disappointment, although in a different way. Once they have the possibility and the opportunity to intervene in human reproduction, there follows a natural desire to improve things. In all of this, the child who is born as a result of technological intervention is no less worthy of love or respect than any other child. Nonetheless, technology, often unawares, introduces into the act of life-giving elements that do not sit well with the dignity of the human person.

Conscience

In the matter of assisted human reproduction, as in all other matters, each individual must make and be guided by a judgement of conscience. Conscience is sometimes taken to mean personal *opinion*, as opposed to an official institutional position. Properly understood, however, conscience is a judgement,

> made about a particular situation,
> against the background of one's own value system or vision of life,
> based on the best available knowledge of the facts.

The capacity to know good from evil (or right from wrong) is a natural quality with which all normally developed human beings are endowed. It does not depend specifically on religious belief. The making of a judgement of conscience does, however, presuppose some coherent set of values, or vision of life. In the case of a believer, religious faith will be an important element in that vision of life.

Insofar as the quality of a judgement of conscience depends on the level of information available, healthcare professionals have an obligation, as part of their professional responsibility, to ensure that patients are fully informed, in terms that they are capable of understanding. Couples whose infertility is treated by IVF are primarily concerned with having a child. To that extent at least, it can be said that their set of values is oriented in favour of life. It is important that couples who are candidates for treatment be fully informed by the providers of the service as to the implications and consequences of IVF, both for the embryo and for themselves. It is only in the light of such information that a fully free decision can be made about the treatment being proposed.

Assisted Human Reproduction: Facts and Ethical Issues

While law is one of the elements that influence the judgement of conscience of individual members of society, it is not the ultimate determinant of conscience. Its purpose is to ensure that the fundamental rights of some are not infringed upon by the decisions of others. The right to freedom of conscience is a fundamental human right, and is not restricted to private individuals. Healthcare professionals, legislators, and others who serve the public, have both a right and a duty to act in accordance with the judgement of conscience. This judgement is rooted in truth, not in expediency, or in the dynamic of supply and demand.

Chapter 2

Assisted Human Reproduction Current Practice

A. Investigation for and Diagnosis of Infertility

Infertility affects as many as one couple in six.[8] The diagnosis of infertility involves the investigation of both partners.

Possible causes of infertility include:
- Non-ovulation and ovulatory disfunction
- Inadequacy of sperm (low sperm-count, infection, etc.)
- Tubal malfunction (due to previous inflammation, endometriosis, surgery, etc.)
- Cervical hostility; anti-sperm antibodies, etc.
- Psycho-sexual factors
- Unexplained (approx. 20 per cent)

In modern healthcare, significant emphasis is placed on prevention. On-going research, aimed at understanding and classifying the causes of infertility, is an essential element in the overall response to infertility. Such research makes it possible to identify strategies, or lifestyle changes, that may reduce infertility levels, and eventually even eliminate certain types of infertility.

B. Responding to Infertility

Couples who are diagnosed as infertile may be offered help under one of two broad headings, namely curative therapy, and circumventive therapy. Curative therapy seeks to identify and treat the root cause of the infertility, thereby making the couple once more fertile, and enabling them to conceive, without further intervention.

Circumventive therapy assumes that it will not be possible to restore the couple's fertility. Instead, the particular cause, which has been identified, is circumvented. The couple are enabled to have a child but, from a medical point of view, they remain an infertile couple.

Assisted Human Reproduction: Facts and Ethical Issues

C. Curative Therapy

1. NaProTechnology

NaProTechnology is not so much a particular treatment as an approach to treatment, which incorporates elements of fertility awareness, surgery, and drug therapy. The term NaProTechnology refers to the use of Natural Procreative Technologies. To quote one of the leading proponents of the approach:

> It (NaProTechnology) can be defined as a science which devotes its medical, surgical and allied health energies and attention to cooperating with the natural procreative methods and functions. When these mechanisms are working properly, NaProTechnology works co-operatively with them. When these mechanisms are functioning abnormally, NaProTechnology cooperates with the procreative mechanisms in producing a form of treatment which corrects the condition, maintains the human ecology and sustains the procreative potential.[9]

An essential element of NaProTechnology is to identify the time of fertility, using a variation of the ovulation method, *CrM NFP*,[10] so that couples whose fertility is low have the optimum chance of achieving a pregnancy. This is effective in treating both male and female infertility. Where particular defects are identified, which can be treated by surgery or drug therapy, the aim of NaPro is to do this without suppressing or destroying the procreative system or dynamic.

2. Surgery

Laser laparoscope, open laser surgery, and micro-surgery, offer significant possibilities in the treatment of endometriosis and associated pelvic adhesions. Proximal tubal occlusion is treatable by means of micro-surgery. An alternative is the recently developed technique known as *transcervical balloon tuboplasty*, which has proved very promising, offering a success rate of 30 per cent or more.

3. Drug Therapy

A common cause of infertility in women is a disorder of ovulation. Where non-ovulation is at the root of infertility, drug therapy is provided, using clomiphene citrate, or preparations of gonadotrophin, which stimulates the ovaries, and the woman may achieve pregnancy without any further medical intervention. Hilgers comments that most of the drugs currently available have limitations as well as advantages.[11] Clomiphene citrate, for example, although it induces ovulation, tends to inhibit cervical mucus. Medications such as Pergonal and Metrodin, which are used to stimulate ovulation, are associated with high multiple births. Where ovulation stimulation is being used, it is recommended that monitoring be carried out, to prevent hyperstimulation of the ovaries, which may lead to serious complications. Other ovulation-related conditions, which are treatable by means of drug therapy, include *sub-optimal luteal function, androgen excess, and hyperprolactanemia.*

Drug therapy is also used very successfully to treat mucus *abnormalities*. The standard medication used is an oral estrogen, which must be administered with Clomiphene Citrate, to ensure that ovulation is not inhibited. Effective alternatives to this standard treatment include Vitamin B6, Guaiafenesin (which is an expectorant), and ampicillin.[12]

D. CIRCUMVENTIVE THERAPY

Where infertility results from causes other than tubal malfunction, disorder of ovulation, or low sperm count, it is common to suggest assisted reproduction therapy (ART). The methods currently in use include IVF[13], ICSI[14] and IUI.[15] Some centres also use GIFT, or ZIFT,[16] but these are less common.

1. *In Vitro* Fertilisation (IVF)

In vitro fertilisation and tubal surgery have approximately the same success rate (25 per cent), but couples to whom IVF is suited will be those for whom tubal surgery is likely to be less successful. Drugs are used to suppress natural ovarian function, and then the ovary is stimulated by injections of gonadotrophin.

The ova are collected, vaginally, by means of an ultrasound-directed probe, and fertilised in the laboratory. Three embryos are placed in the uterine cavity. This is the optimum number, providing the best chance of pregnancy, while avoiding the complications that might arise if larger numbers were used. In the UK the law limits to three the number of embryos that may be placed in the uterine cavity in any one cycle. Some units now prefer to use two, and achieve the same success rates as were gained previously using three. It is reported that, following successful implantation, the spontaneous abortion rate is not increased. In approximately 75 per cent of cases, however, successful implantation will not occur.

The practice of using more than one embryo in each IVF cycle is generally accepted, three being the number normally considered to be safe and effective. Where three embryos are used, the success rate in terms of pregnancies achieved may be up to 30 per cent. A significant proportion of these are twin pregnancies. In terms of live births, the success rate is of the order of 15-20 per cent. Some sources report that the success rate is not significantly less when frozen embryos are used. This obviously depends to some extent on the technology used. This is constantly being developed.

The above figures, of course, refer to the *success rate of the procedure*. The *embryo-survival* rate is significantly lower. Let us assume that three embryos are used, in each of one hundred IVF cycles, and that thirty pregnancies occur, of which one-third are twin pregnancies. This means that, of the three-hundred embryos placed in the uterine cavity, only forty (or 13 per cent) actually survive to a stage at which pregnancy can be confirmed.[17]

An alternative to the above procedure is what is known as natural-cycle-IVF. As the name suggests, no drugs are used to stimulate the ovary. Ova are harvested at the time of ovulation, fertilised *in vitro* using the husband's sperm, and then placed in the uterine cavity. The success rate using this method is significantly lower (at about 10 per cent), but this reflects a significantly higher rate of survival of the individual embryo. There is no question of surplus embryos being generated. Natural-cycle-IVF can be very tedious and unpredictable. There are, however, some signs that it may be possible in the future to mature ova *in vitro*, thus making the process less time-sensitive.

In Northern Ireland, as in Britain and other jurisdictions, surplus fertilised ova are frozen[18], and may be used in subsequent cycles. With the consent of the biological parents, the law allows for these embryos to be placed in the womb of another woman, or to be used for research purposes. UK law provides for the disposal of unused embryos after a period of five years in storage.

In some IVF units, it appears that the practice has developed of transferring as many as five embryos to the uterus, and performing embryo reduction at a later stage. This process of 'un-natural selection' obviously has serious ethical implications.

In the Republic of Ireland, there is no law specifically governing IVF, but the *Guide to Ethical Conduct and Behaviour* includes a requirement that 'any fertilised ovum must be used for normal implantation and must not be deliberately destroyed.'[19] It had been publicly alleged, and never denied, prior to the promulgation of the current *Guide,* that in Ireland, surplus embryos, while not being destroyed, were frequently placed in the cervix rather than in the uterine cavity.

2. Intra-Cytoplasmic Sperm Injection (ICSI)

This is the most recently developed method for by-passing the problem of infertility. It is similar in many ways to IVF. The difference is that each ovum is injected with a single sperm cell. ICSI ensures the penetration by the sperm of the outer layer of the ovum and, therefore, facilitates the beginning of fertilisation. Practitioners recommend this method in cases where regular IVF has failed, and particularly in cases involving oligozoospermia (low sperm count), or where sperm is not ejaculated naturally. Recent literature from Bourn Hall Clinic indicates that 'there is emerging evidence of genetic abnormalities associated with male infertility' and advises careful screening before embarking on ICSI.[20]

3. Embryo Donation

Couples who have previously undergone the process of IVF, and who decide that their family is now complete, may still have surplus embryos in storage. Clinics in some countries are now facilitating embryo donation, whereby these surplus embryos are made available for couples for whom IVF itself has not been succesful, but for whom embryo transfer is a possibility.

In the UK there is a government proposal that children of IVF where embryo donation (or indeed the donation of sperm or ovum), is concerned, will have the right at the age of eighteen to have information about their donor parent(s). As already suggested, this right, if accepted, would conflict with the current practice of guaranteeing anonymity to the donor.

4. Gamete Intra-Fallopian Tube Transfer (GIFT)

In the case of GIFT, a maximum of three ova are selected, and replaced in the fallopian tube, almost immediately after collection, together with a small sample of sperm. Fertilisation actually takes place *in vivo.* This procedure requires the use of

Assisted Human Reproduction: Facts and Ethical Issues

laparoscopy, and involves general anaesthetic. Because this method involves placement of the gametes in the fallopian tubes, it requires that the woman has healthy tubes. The method works well for couples with unexplained infertility, and mild endometriosis. The best results reported indicate a 26 per cent live birth rate.

5. Egg Donation

Egg donation has been common practice for several years. The procedure for obtaining the ovum is the same as in the case of IVF, except that the ova are harvested from a woman other than the one who will conceive and carry the baby. A woman who is herself a candidate for IVF might be asked to donate ova that are surplus to her own requirements. Alternatively, a woman who is a candidate for tubal ligation, or other gynaecological surgery, might be asked to donate her ova prior to surgery.

6. Surrogacy

Surrogacy is an arrangement whereby a woman agrees to conceive a child and carry it to term, on behalf of another woman who, for whatever reason, is unable or unwilling to become pregnant herself. Theoretically surrogacy may involve the use of ova provided by the intended social mother, or by the surrogate.

7. Assisted Insemination by Husband (AIH) *homologous* and Intra-Uterine Insemination (IUI)

Assisted Insemination, which was in use long before IVF, is now less commonly used, as it has little effect in resolving infertility due to sperm deficiency. AIH does offer the possibility of achieving pregnancy in cases where men cannot achieve or sustain erection, or where women have difficulties with vaginismus. Theoretically, this does not necessarily require any medical intervention.

Where the woman is ovulating normally (or will respond to drug therapy), and where the male partner's sperm is satisfactory, problems may still arise because of the inability of the sperm to penetrate the cervical mucus of the female partner. This can be overcome by a procedure known as intra-uterine insemination (IUI), which is a specific variation of AI. Ovulation is induced, and sperm is placed high in the uterus, by means of a catheter, thus avoiding the cervical mucus. IUI can also be used with reasonable success to treat sub-fertility caused by mild endometriosis. Where super-ovulatory drugs are used to stimulate ovum ripening, it is different from IVF in that the objective is to produce three ova, and no more.

8. Artificial Insemination by Donor (AID)

heterologous

This procedure is rarely offered nowadays. The donor has to have a full screening for hepatitis, AIDS, syphilis, etc. Counselling of the donor is easy. It may be more difficult for the couple, however, to accept a situation in which only one of them will be the natural parent of the child.

9. Testicular Biopsy

Testicular biopsy is a surgical proceedure by means of which sperm are extracted directly from the testicles. This procedure is considered to be of benefit in cases where the male has a sperm count below 1 million. Its availability further reduces the need/demand for AID. Sperms can be obtained in this way and used for ICSI. Drug treatment for reduced sperm count has been largely abandoned.

We can now go on to evaluate the therapeutic procedures outlined in Chapter 2, in the light of the basic principles established in Chapter 1.

Assisted Human Reproduction: Facts and Ethical Issues

Chapter 3

Assisted Human Reproduction

Ethical Evaluation of Current Practice

A. Curative Therapy

1. NaProTechnology

As an approach to treatment NaProTechnology invariably involves natural (or *in vivo*) fertilisation. It does not, therefore, place embryos at risk to their life or bodily integrity. NaPro fosters dialogue and co-operation between the couple, with its emphasis on fertility awareness. The emphasis on respect for the natural reproductive process means that NaPro is consistent with the meaning and integrity of human sexuality.

Evaluation
NaProTechnology is consistent with all three of the ethical principles proposed in Chapter 1.

2. Surgery

All surgical intervention is governed by the principle of totality. The element of risk involved is acceptable insofar as it is in proportion to the positive outcome anticipated. There are no ethical difficulties specifically associated with the surgical treatment of infertility. The fact that surgery may be required to restore tubal function that has been damaged by sterilisation, and that this surgery may not always be successful, does serve as a reminder that tubal ligation as a contraceptive method is invasive of bodily integrity, and should not be carried out unless it is medically indicated.

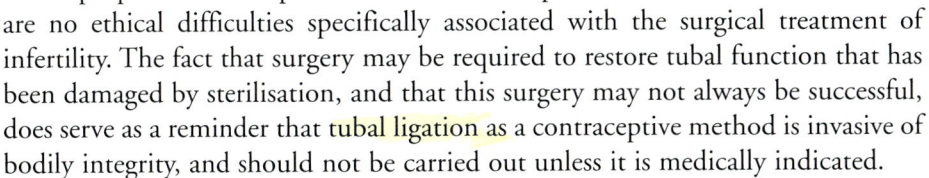

Evaluation
This form of treatment is ethically acceptable under all three headings.

3. Drug Treatment

The use of drug therapy to stimulate ovulation seems to be perfectly acceptable from an ethical point of view, provided always that the patient is adequately informed and consents to the treatment. The use of clomiphene or gonadotrophin preparations assists rather than replaces the natural reproductive function. Where the stimulation of ovulation is brought about with a view to IVF or ICSI, the ethical issue relates not so much to the harvesting of large quantities of ova, but to the way in which they are subsequently used. The possible effect of the drug treatment on the mother must also be taken into account in arriving at an ethical evaluation.

Assisted Human Reproduction: Facts and Ethical Issues

Evaluation

This form of treatment, used with discretion, is ethically acceptable under all three headings.

B. Circumventive Therapy

1. *In Vitro* Fertilisation and Embryo Transfer

Depending on how it is carried out, the ethical problems posed by *in vitro* fertilisation and embryo transfer may be minimised, but they are so rooted in its very nature that it is very difficult to provide IVF effectively without going down a path that inevitably leads to the death of a great proportion of human embryos.

a. Research

It is widely accepted that if IVF is to be developed, on-going embryo research is inevitable. IVF also affords the possibility of research on embryos, which might help to discover the causes and possible cures for genetic abnormalities. The Warnock Committee, set up to make recommendations to the British Government, approved embryo research, with only three out of sixteen members opposed. A further four members opposed the generation of embryos specifically for research.

In Ireland, destructive embryo research is prohibited by the ethical guidelines of the Medical Council. The *Guide to Ethical Conduct and Behaviour* also specifically excludes the generation of embryos for research purposes.[21] The fact remains, however, that IVF, as practised in Ireland, is dependent on research that is going on elsewhere, and will continue to be dependent on this research in the future.

Insofar as human embryos cannot themselves consent to be the subjects of research, no research of any kind may be carried out without the consent of parents or legal guardians. The fundamental principle applying to proxy-consent of this kind is that only research that holds out the realistic possibility of therapeutic benefit for the embryo concerned may be permitted. A judgement as to the appropriateness of any experimental procedure involves weighing the likely benefits for the individual against the risks involved in the procedure.

b. The use of multiple embryos

Every human individual is a value in himself or herself. As noted above, the practice of multiple embryo replacement involves accepting that the survival rate per embryo is in inverse proportion to the likelihood of achieving pregnancy. In effect, therefore, IVF contributes to an ethos that regards the embryo as a means to an end, rather than as a value in and for itself.

c. The storage and disposal of embryos

The generation of excess embryos gives rise to an ethical dilemma. The moral issue is related to the taking of an initial decision, the consequences and implications of which can be reasonably foreseen. The decision in question is the decision to generate more embryos than can safely be placed in the uterus in one cycle. This decision is not inevitable in IVF, but tends to be made for pragmatic reasons. Once it has been made, further difficult choices seem to follow inevitably. It would seem that, if IVF is to be developed in a way that is both highly efficient *and* consistent with respect for life, the focus will need to be on the discovery of some successful means of freezing the ovum. In the absence of such a possibility, serious ethical problems remain.

The freezing and storage of embryos appears on the surface to be more acceptable than their use for research, or their immediate disposal. Storage holds out the hope that these embryos may, in time, also be used to overcome infertility, either in the natural parents, or in other couples with the parents' consent. Storage is not, however, a satisfactory solution, for a number of reasons.

Human fertilisation is a dynamic process rather than an instantaneous occurrence. The human pro-nucleus is undoubtedly more than simply a sperm and an ovum. Indeed, by this stage, the action of the sperm, as has been noted, has already had a significant impact on the ovum. There is no sound basis for treating the human pro-nucleus as deserving any less respect than the human embryo after the completion of fertilisation.

Storage, of its very nature, is temporary. Embryos, while in storage, are vulnerable to interference, and are impeded from attaining their natural end. The Human Embryology Authority in the UK has determined a maximum storage time of five years for embryos, after which time they must be disposed of. This procedure has already been carried out, involving the destruction of huge numbers of unwanted embryos. The fact that such a process is clinical and painless does not fundamentally change the reality.

Assisted Human Reproduction: Facts and Ethical Issues

The *Guide to Ethical Conduct and Behaviour* specifically requires that 'any fertilised ovum must be used for normal implantation and must not be deliberately destroyed.'[22] The practice of replacing surplus embryos outside the cavity of the uterus where they cannot survive is, to all intents and purposes, the same as the disposal of embryos, and is quite clearly not acceptable within the terms of the *Guide*. The guide excludes 'the creation of new forms of life for experimental purposes, or the deliberate and intentional destruction of human life already formed.'

The *Guide* expressly states that there is 'no objection to the preservation of sperm or ova to be used subsequently on behalf of those from whom they were originally taken,' but makes no reference to the freezing and storing of embryos (the ethical implications of which are far more significant), or to the criteria to be applied should such a procedure be undertaken.[23] Contrary to what has been suggested by some commentators, therefore, there is no basis whatsoever for suggesting that the Medical Council has accepted or approved the freezing of embryos. Regrettably the same cannot be said for a new ethical code promulgated by the Institute of Obstetricians and Gynaecologists in July 1999.

d. A technological process
IVF is a tightly controlled and highly technological process. It is a process in which the role of scientists and doctors tends to take precedence over the role of the parents themselves. In the normal course of events, a technological process has its own internal logic, which includes quality control, and which is sensitive to the fluctuations of the market-place.

The human embryo is far more than simply a commodity, even a very valuable one. Apart altogether from the physical risk to the embryo, which follows from the selective nature of the process, we must question whether such a highly technological process is a suitable vehicle for the love and the mystery which, properly speaking, is so central to the generation of a human person.

Evaluation
IVF, as normally practised, is inconsistent with respect for the life and bodily integrity of the embryo. In many cases it is inconsistent with respect for the family and the identity of origin of the child. With regard to the integrity of human sexuality, IVF is, to say the least, intrusive.

2. Intra-Cytoplasmic Sperm Injection (ICSI)

This sperm injection procedure is a major advance from a technological point of view. From an ethical point of view, however, it is subject to exactly the same limitations as IVF. Once again, although the process is different, a key moral issue hinges on the decision about whether or not surplus embryos will be generated, and what will happen to them.

Testicular biopsy is an invasive procedure, and this should also be taken into account in any ethical evaluation. It is also worth noting that ICSI makes it possible to respond to infertility in men with severe sperm abnormalities. In the course of natural fertilisation, the individual sperm that ultimately fertilises an ovum has survived a process of natural selection, and achieved first place in a competition of millions. Even in IVF, some degree of natural selection has occured. In ICSI, however, the chosen sperm has no competition. This in itself may be a contributory factor in genetic malformation. The health of future generations requires, therefore, that appropriate research be carried out to establish that genetic abnormalities are not being transmitted through the use of ICSI.

Evaluation
From an ethical point of view, ICSI brings with it the same problems as IVF.

3. Embryo Donation

In many jurisdictions, subsequent to IVF or ICSI, it is common practice for surplus embryos to be used, with the consent of the natural parents, to provide children for other infertile couples. It must be said at the outset that to allow surplus embryos to survive in this way is infinitely preferable to disposing of them, or making use of them as objects of research. This is not to say, however, that there are no ethical implications involved.

The practice of placing an embryo or embryos in the uterus of a woman who is not the natural mother, and in the care of parents who are not the natural parents, does separate parenthood from the responsibility of care. It creates a whole new complex relationship, in which family is redefined to include two sets of parents. This inevitably gives scope for some confusion about the identity of the child who will be born.

Assisted Human Reproduction: Facts and Ethical Issues

Parents may, of course, die or separate. Children may be born to and brought up by single mothers. They may be adopted. None of these circumstances lessens in any way the dignity of the child. There is a fundamental difference, however, between responding constructively and lovingly to a child who already exists (in or out of the womb) and deliberately creating a situation in which a child's sense of identity and family membership is blurred. What is significant, once again, is the initial decision to generate surplus embryos, a decision that is taken in isolation from any coherent plan for the future personal care of the human individuals concerned.

Evaluation
Taken in isolation, embryo donation respects the right to life and bodily integrity of the embryo. It is inconsistent, however, with respect for the family and the identity of origin of the child.

4. GIFT

Insofar as GIFT involves fertilisation *in vivo*, it does not involve many of the ethical difficulties that are associated with IVF. It does not involve the storage of 'surplus' embryos. It does, however, expose the woman to the risk of repeating the harvesting of ova, if no pregnancy is achieved in the first cycle. In many centres, also, IVF tends to be a fall-back position in the event that GIFT fails, using the surplus ova obtained.

Evaluation
GIFT does respect the life and bodily integrity of the embryo. It is arguably less intrusive in terms of the integrity of sexuality, because it does not totally remove the element of mystery and the randomness of natural fertilisation. It does, however, replace the act of intercourse, rather than assisting it, and for that reason is not morally acceptable.

5. Artificial Insemination by Husband (AIH), and Intra-Uterine Insemination (IUI)

Artificial insemination with the husband's sperm is, relatively speaking, non-intrusive. The main cause of concern might be the manner in which the sperm is obtained. If sperm is obtained by means of masturbation, and particularly where pornographic stimulation is used, the issue is one of human dignity. If, as is now more common, testicular biopsy is used, the issue is one of the proportion between risk and benefit, as in the case of all surgery. Some obstetricians have drawn attention to the fact that there is no reason why any person other than the couple needs to be involved in AIH.

IUI, insofar as it involves a certain degree of technology, is somewhat more intrusive than AIH. Otherwise, the issues are the same.

Evaluation
The principles of respect for life, and respect for the family, are both respected by AIH and IUI. Strictly speaking, AIH and IUI do not respect the integrity of the sexual act, even if its intrusiveness is significantly less that in some other procedures.

6. Artificial Insemination by Donor (AID)

In the case of AID, the child to be born will, at least, be born of the biological mother. On the male side, however, the link between paternity and the exercise of fatherly care is broken. The fact that one of the couple is a biological parent and the other is not can create its own tensions in the family.

AID also requires careful screening of donors to ensure that there is no risk of the transmission of Hepatitis, HIV, or genetic defects. Once the principle of the screening of donors is accepted, logic would suggest that donors should also be selected for their positive genetic characteristics.

Evaluation
AID respects the right to life and bodily integrity of the embryo/child. It is inconsistent, however, with respect for the family, and identity of origin of the child. It does not respect the meaning and integrity of sexuality.

7. Ovum Donation

The ethical issues involved in the case of ovum donation are the same as those involved in AID, except that, in this case, it is the father who will be the natural parent.

Evaluation
Taken in isolation, the ethical evaluation of ovum donation is the same as that which applies in the case of AID. If the donation of ova takes place in the context of IVF, however, other issues arise, as outlined above.

Assisted Human Reproduction: Facts and Ethical Issues

8. Surrogacy

Surrogacy can, theoretically, take various forms. The surrogate is usually also the biological mother (i.e., she also provides the ovum that is used). Alternatively, her womb may simply be made available for a period of time between IVF and birth. Insofar as respect for the identity of origin is concerned, the difficulty is that the surrogate mother is outside the partnership of marriage, and will not be the parent in any on-going sense. There is also sufficient anecdotal evidence to show that the bonding that takes place between a surrogate mother and the child in her womb, can and does give rise to situations in which the child subsequently becomes the victim of a struggle for custody between the surrogate and the intended social parents. This is all the more likely in cases in which the surrogate is also the biological mother. From a legal point of view, it is the woman who bears the child who is recognised as the mother.

Evaluation

Surrogacy is inconsistent with the meaning and integrity of human sexuality. If it involves the donation of the ovum by the surrogate, it is also inconsistent with respect for the family and the identity of origin of the child. IVF, if it is involved, adds other issues as outlined above.

9. Assisted Reproductive Therapy and Marriage

Due regard both for the dignity of a possible child, and for the central role of the family in society, makes it particularly inappropriate that IVF or artificial insemination should be available outside subsisting marriage.

Chapter 4

Healthcare Policy and Assisted Human Reproduction

1. Legislating for AHR

As suggested above, the purpose of law in relation to healthcare policy, as in any other area of social life, is not to restrict freedoms *per se*, but to ensure that the exercise of freedom by some does not constitute an obstacle to the legitimate freedom of others. Where healthcare is concerned, law can be taken to include constitutional provision, positive law, and also such self-regulation as is devolved by the state to the professional bodies governing the various healthcare professions.

We have already considered three important principles in relation to the provision of assisted human reproduction therapy, namely respect for the right to life and bodily integrity, respect for the identity of origin, and respect for the essential meaning of human sexuality. In the Republic of Ireland, the absence of any legislative framework, which would govern the way in which these rights are to be vindicated, is unsatisfactory.

2. Funding

IVF and ICSI are expensive procedures. Clinics providing them at the present time are essentially self-funding, and operate on a commercial basis. The clients are expected to cover their own costs. For those who cannot afford to meet these costs, the units usually operate on a non profit-making basis, thereby facilitating some of these clients. It is only reasonable, however, to assume that couples whose costs are beyond their means do not in general have access to these IVF or similar programmes. Whether, and on what terms, the state should provide funding for these patients is no doubt a contentious issue.

As in the case of any medical condition, couples are entitled to have their possible infertility investigated and treated. This entitlement is, of course, not an absolute one. There is relatively little difficulty in offering investigation and diagnosis to any couple that appears to need it. Responding to the diagnosis is more problematic, not simply because of the implications in relation to the respect for life, and for the identity of origin, but also because healthcare funding is limited. Those who are responsible for administering healthcare funding, (e.g., health boards and the administrators of individual hospitals), are ethically obliged to ensure that resources are allocated in accordance with the most urgent need, and to make that allocation on some objective basis.

For purposes of cost analysis, the diagnosis of and response to infertility could be divided under a number of headings, as follows:
- the cost of investigation and diagnosis (hormone profiles and routine semen analysis)
- the cost of drug therapy (whether on its own, or as part of IVF, etc.)
- the cost of IVF and ET, or ICSI
- the cost of the hospital stay.

a.   Investigation and diagnosis
Hospital admission for laparoscopy, ultrasound, etc. is at present organised on a waiting list basis, does not receive any priority to an emergency admission, and is subject to cancellation. Costs of such investigation are funded either by the hospital, or by the patient's own health insurance. Both VHI and BUPA cover investigation.

b.   Drug therapy
Drug therapy as a treatment for infertility is currently available on the same basis as any other form of drug therapy, with public patients covered by public health schemes, and private patients covered by their health insurance. Both VHI and BUPA cover drug therapy.

c.   IVF and ICSI
IVF units in Ireland are usually situated within the confines of a general hospital campus. They are responsible for the provision, funding, and training of their own staff. IVF and ICSI are not available on public health schemes, nor are they currently covered by VHI or BUPA.

d.   Hospital stay
Where hospital stay is required, it is not clear how the costs would be covered. If the stay is directly linked to the provision of IVF or similar procedures, it is unlikely to be covered by health insurance. Unless the centre providing treatment is essentially self-sufficient, and has its own dedicated facilities, the provision of in-hospital treatment will inevitably have an impact on the bed status, theatre space, and other facilities of the hospital.

The difficulties in relation to funding of IVF and similar procedures are two-fold. If the treatment of infertility were to be publicly funded, this would have implications for the resourcing of other services. If the position remains that the cost must be borne by the couple seeking treatment, then high-cost methods of responding to infertility will be exclusively available to the better-off sectors of society.

If it were decided to allocate public funding to procedures such as IVF and ICSI, it would be necessary to establish just and reasonable criteria to govern the selection of candidates for treatment. Among the issues to be considered would be marital status and age. It would be very easy to envisage how other criteria, such as economic status and emotional stability might eventually find their way into the equation.

Clearly, there comes a point when, after a number of unsuccessful attempts, it is important to consider, not only in terms of resources, but also in terms of the impact on the couple, whether it is appropriate to continue trying to achieve pregnancy.

3. The Priority of Prevention and Cure

The highest profile in relation to the care of infertile couples is given to procedures that essentially circumvent rather than cure infertility. While this may be the area of highest public awareness and highest level of demand, the areas of prevention and cure should not be neglected in public policy and in the allocation of resources. If, as seems to be the case, infertility is on the increase, it should be possible to establish how this is related to lifestyle and environment. Two obvious areas for study are:
- change in patterns of sexual activity, including sexually transmitted diseases and contraception,[24]
- changes in work patterns and associated stress levels.

Assisted Human Reproduction: Facts and Ethical Issues

Appendix

Notes

Select Bibliography

NOTES

1. United Nations Organisation, *Universal Declaration of Human Rights* (New York, 1948), #3.
2. The first visual evidence of the pro-nuclear stage is the presence of two circles in the organism, about 16-20 hours after fertilisation. Syngamy comes about 5 hours later.
3. Balinski, B. I., *An Introduction to Embryology* (New York: CBS, 1981), 112.
4. Several centres in England have been given permission to store ova by freezing and, in one recent case, permission has been given to use a frozen ovum in an IVF programme.
5. It will be helpful to deal briefly with some of the arguments put forward by those who suggest that it is not necessary to afford personal rights to the embryo until some weeks after fertilisation.

    Totopotentiality of cells: It is not clear until the pregnancy is established, which cells will actually become the embryo, and which will become the placenta, chorion, etc. This is not particularly relevant to the issue of respect. All of the cells are essential to the existence of the embryo at the time. Equally none of the cells that are present in the first few days survive through to birth. Personal identity is not dependent on the survival of individual cells.

    Twinning and Re-combination: It is argued that, in the early days of pregnancy, the organism may divide and/or re-combine. The organic mechanisms of monozygotic twinning are not fully understood, but there are good indications that they are genetic, and that certain organisms contain the potential for this kind of twinning, *ab initio*. A new human organism, on coming into existence, would have its own substantial form (or soul). The soul is, of course, a metaphysical rather than a physical reality, and is not itself subject to the laws of biology.

    The death of any living creature involves the separation of body and soul. It is reasonable to suggest that, on the 'death' of a twin in the very first days after fertilisation, biological material may be absorbed by the remaining organism. The possibility of twinning and re-combination does not change the reality that the early embryo (or zygote) is a living being, generated and growing as a whole.

Assisted Human Reproduction: Facts and Ethical Issues

The so-called primitive streak simply marks the latest stage at which monozygotic twinning can take place. If, as suggested above, monozygotic twinning is genetically based, then we have no reason to believe it hasn't begun earlier, simply because we haven't seen it earlier.

6. *Universal Declaration of Human Rights,* # 16.
7. Congregation for the Doctrine of the Faith, *Donum Vitae (Instruction on Respect for Human Life in its Origin and on the Dignity of Procreation),* # 1 (Vatican City: Libreria Editrice Vaticana, 1987).
8. The term infertility is used here to refer to the inability of a couple to conceive for two years.
9. Thomas W. Hilgers, *Medical Applications of Natural Family Planning* (Omaha: Pope Paul VI Institute Press, 1991), xi.
10. Creighton Model, Natural Family Planning.
11. Cf. Thomas W. Hilgers, op. cit., 143.
12. Ibid.
13. IVF (& ET) = In-Vitro Fertilisation and Embryo Transfer.
14. ICSI = Intra-cytoplasmic sperm injection.
15. Intra-Uterine Insemination.
16. Gamete Intra-Fallopian Tube Transfer, and Zygote Intra-Fallopian Tube Transfer, respectively.
17. Cf. Luno, A.F. and R.L. Mondejar, *La Fecondazione In Vitro* (Rome: Citta Nuova, 1986), 85.
18. The technical term used for this procedure is *cryopreservation.*
19. Irish Medical Council, *Guide to Ethical Conduct and Behaviour,* # 26.4. (Dublin: Irish Medical Council, 1998).
20. Bourn Hall Clinic, *Update* (Winter 1997), 5.
21. Irish Medical Council, op. cit., # 26.1
22. Ibid., # 26.4.
23. Ibid., # 26.3.
24. Some research has been done which indicates that the use of artificial hormones has a serious effect on fertility (cf. Dr Ellen Grant, *Sexual Chemistry – Understanding our Hormones, the Pill and HRT.* Cedar Paperback, 1994). The risk of infection related to the use of IUCD has also been documented.

SELECT BIBLIOGRAPHY

ASHLEY, Benedict and Kevin O'ROURKE. *Healthcare Ethics: A Theological Analysis.* St Louis, Missouri: UPA, 1978.

AUSTRALIAN SENATE SELECT COMMITTEE. *Human Embryo Experimentation in Australia.* Canberra: Australian Government Publishing Service, 1986.

CONGREGATION for the DOCTRINE of the FAITH. *Donum vitae.* Vatican City: Libreria Editrice Vaticana, 1987.

DORAN, Kevin. *What is a Person?* New York: Edwin Mellen Press, 1989.

_____. 'Person – A Key Concept for Ethics.' *Linacre Quarterly.* Elm Grove, Wisconsin: November 1989.

_____. 'Dilemmas Posed by IVF and the Surplus Embryos,' *Irish Medical Times,* 12 November 1993, 18.

DUIGNAN, Niall. 'The Treatment of Infertility: Ethical Issues.' In *Ethical Issues in Reproductive Medicine,* edited by Maurice Reidy. Dublin: Gill and Macmillan, 1982.

FLEMING, J. and T. IGLESIAS. 'Human Fertilisation In-Vitro, compared with Nature.' *The Lancet* (1985), 1.

GRANT, Ellen. *Sexual Chemistry – Understanding our Hormones, the Pill and HRT.* Cedar Paperback, 1994.

HARRIS, John. 'In Vitro Fertilisation: The Ethical Issues'. *The Philosophical Quarterly,* vol 33, no. 132 (July 1983), 217-237.

HALBROOK, David. 'Medical Ethics and the Potentialities of the Living Being.' *British Medical Journal* (August 1985), 459-462.

HILGERS, T. W. *Medical Applications of Natural Family Planning*. Omaha: Pope Paul VI Institute Press, 1991.

IGLESIAS, Teresa. 'In Vitro Fertilisation: the Major Issues.' *Journal of Medical Ethics* (1984), 1, 32-37.

_____. 'What Kind of Being is the Human Embryo.' *Ethics and Medicine* (1986), 2:1, 2-7.

MURRAY, Donal. *A Question of Morality: Christian Morality and In Vitro Fertilisation*. (Paper delivered at the Glenstal Ecumenical Conference). Dublin: Veritas, 1985.

TEICHMANN, Jenny. 'The Definition of a Person.' *Philosophy* 60, 175-185.

WARNOCK, Mary. 'In Vitro Fertilisation: The Ethical Issues.' *The Philosophical Quarterly*, vol. 33, 132 (July 1983), 238-249.

WARNOCK, Mary, ed. *A Question of Life*. Oxford: Basil Blackwell, 1985.